1000
CORNISH PLACE NAMES
EXPLAINED

Julyan Holmes

TOR MARK PRESS REDRUTH

DEDICATION

**Dhe'm karadow, Loveday, may kavav kerensa,
kennerth ha govenek.**

First published 1983 by Dyllansow Truran

This edition published by

**Tor Mark Press
United Downs Ind. Est. St Day Redruth
Cornwall TR16 5HY**

Design by Ray Lancefield
info@thedesignfield.com

Printed in Cornwall by R.Booth (Bookbinder) Ltd & Troutbeck Press,
Antron Hill, Mabe, Penryn TR10 9HH

ISBN 0 85025 380 2

ACKNOWLEDGEMENT

*It would have been quite impossible to compile this
book were it not for the work of scholars who have
carried out research in this field before me. My thanks
go to these and to others whose advice has been
invaluable but who should on no account be held
responsible for any errors.*

FOREWORD

Cornwall's strange, mellifluous place names give it a flavour quite different from English counties. Many must wonder where they all came from.

This book is designed to help not only the bewildered stranger but also the born Cornishman who may have taken them for granted since childhood.

Our abandoned engine-houses and deserted coves, so beloved by romantics, are a constant reminder of a way of life now gone, when copper, fish and tin gave thousands of Cornishmen and women their livelihood In just the same way, once you know the secret, our place-names open the door to a new language and, in fact, to a whole Celtic civilisation which is the true heritage of *KERNOW.*

Renewed awareness of Cornwall's submerged identity has led to a growing interest in its celtic heritage. Every year, more and more people are introduced to the Cornish language, both in and out of school. While not all will go on to speak it fluently, they naturally wish to make sense of those words of Cornish that we all use every day – words which many bear as their surnames.

For place-names are as much part of the language as the words for 'butter' or 'cheese'. In fact, if you browse through the pages of this book, you will soon find that you have learnt a dozen or so words and their meanings.

Out of the thousands of Cornish place-names, I have only been able to include one thousand, mainly the names of towns, villages and farms, with a sprinkling of coastal names and a few others of special interest.

Although the vast majority of farms are named in Cornish, there are, for historical reasons, some in French, many in English (and Old English) and even some with a little Latin! The only English names included are those which might be mistaken for Cornish.

Inevitably, in such a long list, every name cannot always be fully explained: sometimes they contain forgotten or unrecognised words but, much more often, specially in those beginning *Bos, Car, Lan, Res* or *Tre,* the second part is an old Celtic personal name. Such names were given a thousand or more years ago and probably had no more meaning to the medieval Cornish-speaker than does the name Alfred to a present-day Englishman.

Some better-known examples of personal names, enough to give you the 'feel' of them, can be found on page 14.

A LITTLE HISTORY

The Cornish language is directly descended from the Celtic of ancient Gaul and pre-Roman Britain, so we can say that it has been spoken here for more than two thousand years. Its closest relatives are Welsh and Breton and it has a kinship with Irish, Scottish and Manx Gaelic.

After the Roman Empire collapsed, shortly after 400 AD, English (or Saxon) settlers from North Germany began to overrun the island. By 800 AD, the British language was confined to Cornwall, Wales, Cumbria, South Scotland and Brittany (where it had been taken by emigrants from the south west).

During the ninth and tenth centuries, Cornwall fell under the sway of the powerful kings of Wessex. Saxons settled in the north and east especially north of Bude, where Cornish names are scarce. Outside this area, English -ton added to Cornish names, marks their colonial centres, but the Cornish people continued to use their own language.

At about this time, Cornish and Welsh began to go their own separate ways, though, even today, many of our place names are instantly recognisable to a Welshman. This is even more true for Breton since that language remained identical for centuries more. Shortly after, the Normans came, adding French to the language mix. Old Cornish was transformed into Middle Cornish. The most obvious change was of t into s in many words, such as cuit – a wood (compare Welsh coed) which became koes (or cos).

Throughout the Middle Ages, Cornish retreated westwards under the pressure of English. In 1400, Cornish could have been heard everywhere west of a line from Tintagel to Looe. By the time of the Reformation (c. 1540), it had disappeared east of Bodmin, though, further west English was hardly known outside the towns.

Up to then, religious or 'miracle' plays, performed in Cornish in a Plen an Gwari or open-air theatre, had done much to keep the language alive. The new Anglican churchmen did not approve of them and they fell into disuse. When the pro-Catholic Prayerbook Rebellion of 1549 was defeated, many Cornishmen (whose fathers had twice marched against English armies) were 'persuaded' to adopt English ways. History was to prove that learning English did little to improve the lot of the Cornish peasant!

Even so, long after this, some Cornishmen so resented the foreigners that they would reply to an enquiry in English,

"My ny vynnav kows sowsnek" "I will not speak English"!

Nevertheless another century saw Cornish driven west of Truro, where, its literature forgotten, it lingered on the lips of fishermen until about 1800, and faded from the scene, as did the last chough a century or so later, on the very edge of the Atlantic cliffs.

Fortunately the seeds of revival had already been sown, and, after a period of ignominy, Cornish is again on the lips of Cornishmen.

THE SPELLING OF PLACE NAMES

At the time when most Cornish literature was being composed, roughly between 1400 and 1600, the spelling was at least as regular as contemporary English, but, as Cornish was abandoned bit by bit, so the spelling became more and more erratic.

As a general rule, the later the date of the record, the worse the spelling. For that reason *it is no use looking in a dictionary for the meaning of a traditional place name.* It is vital to look at older spellings before trying to interpret them.

Apart from the irregular and anglicised spellings, some coastal names have even been respelt by chart-makers as Welsh! There are several changes in pronunciation which are reflected in writing. Because the language passed out of use later in the west than in the east, names are preserved in an older form on Bodmin Moor than at Land's End.

Penquite, *Pen cuit,* is found further west as Pencoose, *Penn koes,* with the same meaning, "end of the wood". An even later development turned *Pen* into *Pedn* and *Crom* (curved) into *Crobben.* This affected several other words as well.

Besides these historical changes, there are also some regular ones caused by Celtic grammar. Known as 'mutations', these rules mean that the first letter of some words in certain set positions must change into another.

By these rules, B and M both become V, D becomes Th (strictly Dh), C and K become G, G becomes W or else disappears, P becomes B and T becomes D. In place names only, F will appear as V, and S as Z.

These changes are found with feminine nouns after *An* (the) and with other words placed immediately after feminine nouns, (all nouns in Cornish are classed as either masculine or feminine).

For example, 'The Upper Farm' in Cornish is *An dre wartha,* made up of *An+tre+gwartha.*

Another point of interest is that many words ending *-ow* are plurals.

Finally, since these names were passed on by word of mouth from generation to generation, they often become distorted in ways which do not follow any rules.

Some words are mistaken for one another; in particular there is a tendency for many words to end up as Tre, Pol or Lan. Also, R and N are both liable to become L, especially at the beginning of a name, while R and S are often interchanged in middle position. C (K) is also liable to be exchanged for T, while amongst vowel sounds, perhaps the most significant alteration is that of yr (ir) and er to ar at the beginning of a name, as with all those starting Car- (which were originally Ker-).

Other examples of such changes can be spotted in the word-lists on pages 12-40 where I have put together many of the commonest words found in place names with some of the strange forms thay have taken.

A LITTLE GRAMMAR

A casual glance shows that Cornish is not a bit like English. The words are unfamiliar, and so is the grammar, which is in many ways more like French than English.

In particular, Cornish, like French, generally puts the adjective (or describing word) after the noun, Instead of in front of it as in English. In the name *Men hir,* (long stone), the Cornish words *men* (stone) and *hir* (long) are in the opposite order to the English.

In the same way, where English says Johnston (John's town), Cornish says *Trejowan* (where *Tre* means 'town').

Other describing words also follow the main noun: in the name Rose-an-Grouse (*Ros an grows*) meaning 'Cross Heath', the Cornish reads word for word "heath (of) the cross". (The word 'of ' is not needed in the Cornish.)

Of course there are exceptions, since, just as in French, some adjectives are frequently placed before the noun. The main ones are the colours *gwynn,* white, *rudh,* red, *gwyrdh,* green and *melyn,* yellow, plus *hen,* old, *berr,* short, *hir,* long and *moel,* bare.

PRONUNCIATION

In nearly every case the traditional pronunciation of place names still points to its meaning, and it is a great pity when the accent is misplaced.

Just as in English one says "Longstone" with the stress on *Long.* so Cornish stresses the same word in "Menheere" (*Men hir*), with the stress on "heere". For this reason most two-syllable place names are stressed on the second part, while longer names are stressed on the next-to-last syllable.

The common pattern can be remembered by thinking of the words "Resign" and "Tremendous" (both of which could easily appear on a Cornish map).

Most exceptions are equally logical: Hendra, Gwendreath, *Gwynndreth,* Harlyn, *Hirlynn,* etc., all stressed on the first part, or Menadew, *Menydh du,* Canakey, *Karn an ki* etc., all stressed on the last part. It is always the describing element that is emphasised – that is the part of the name which distinguishes that particular hill, farm or beach.

One personal name at least was also stressed on the last syllable: Kenhorn, which is formed in Polkinghorne; and Linkinhorne, and explains the irregular pronunciation of these two names.

Finally beware of traps like Tregony (NOT Tre-goaney but Tregny) which is due to contraction of a longer word. Luxulyan too, is very often mispronounced: the middle *u* represents the sound 'i' as it often does in the Cornish language so that the name rhymes with 'million'. After reading this introduction and looking up the meaning of Cardinham, nobody will dream of calling that place Carding'm.

Common Cornish Words as found in place-names
(dictionary spellings in Italics)

Alls, alt, halt	*als*	-cliff
An	*an*	-the
Bal	*bal*	-mine
Bar	*barr*	-top
Beagle, biggal, bugle	*1. begel. 2. bugel*	-1.small hill -2.shepherd
Bell	*bell (pell)*	-far
Bo, bos, bod, be, bis, bus	*bos*	-dwelling
Bowgie	*bowji*	-cowshed
Brane	*bran*	-crow
Bray, brea	*bre*	-hill
Braze, brawze	*bras*	-big
Burn,	*brynn*	-hill
Car, caer	*ker*	-walled village
Carn, can	*karn*	-rock-pile
Carow	*karow*	-stag
Carrack carrag carrick	*karrek*	-rock
Che, chi, chy, ch-	*chi*	-house
Coose, cos, coys, cus, cut	*koes*	-a wood
Coath, coth	*koth*	-old
Craze	*kres*	-middle
Creeg, creel, crig, creet	*krug*	-mound, barrow
Crows	*krows*	-cross
Deen, din, dun	*din*	-fort
Dennis, dinas	*dinas*	-fort
-dew, -due	*du*	-black
Dour, dower	*dowr*	-water
Dow, do, du	*dew (or fem. diw)*	-two
-dra, -drea	*dra (tre)*	-home
-dreath	*dreth (treth)*	-beach
Drennick, drinnick	*dreynek*	-thorny
-drizzick, -drisack	*dreysek*	-brambly
Eglos, -iglas	*eglos*	-church
En	*an*	-the
Ennis, innis, enys	*ynys*	-island, isolated place
Fenton, fenter	*fenten*	-a spring
Garrack, garrick	*garrek (karrek)*	-rock
Gazick	*gasek (kasek)*	-mare
Gear	*ger (ker)*	-walled village
Gelly, gilly	*gelli (kelli)*	-grove
-gett, -gus, -goose	*goes (koes)*	-a wood
-gey	*ji(chi)*	-house

7

Gew	gew (kew)	-enclosed field
Gon, goon, gun	goen	-downs
Gooth	goedh	-goose
Goth	goth (koth)	-old
Gove	gov	-smith
Gover	gover	-stream
-graze	gres (kres)	-middle
-grean, green, grain	greun (or growynn)	-grain (or gravel)
Greeb, gribba, gribben	grib (krib), gribenn (kribenn)	-crest
Grey	gre	-flock, herd
-grows	grows (krows)	-cross
Gweal	gwel	-cultivated field
Gwen, -gwin, -gwidden	gwynn	-white
Hal, hale, hall, haul, hole	hal	-moor
Har, her, -heer, -hyr	hir	-long
Helligan, hellick	helik, heligenn	-willow(s)
Hels, helles	hellys (hen lys)	-old court
Hen	hen	-old
Henver	henfordh	-old road
Ince, innis	ynys	-island, isolated place
Kelly, killy	kelli	-grove
kernick	kernek	-corner
Kestle	kestell (variant of kastell)	-castle, village
Kie, key	ki	-dog
La, le, lan, lans, lant	nans	-valley
Lan	lann	-holy enclosure
-lay, -lee,	legh	-flat rock
-laze	las (glas)	-green/blue
Les	leys	-mud
Les, us	lys	-court, palace
Lid, us, loose, luz	loes	-grey, hoary
Lidden, un, lyn	lynn	-pool, lake
Loe, looe	logh	-creek, inlet
Main, mayne, mean, men, min	men	-stone
Mellan, molin, bolin	melin	-mill
Min	min	-edge
Mor	mor	-sea
Mul,	moel	-bare
Nan, nance, nans, nant	nans	-valley
Nare	an ardh	-the height
-newth, nouth, noweth, nowth	nowydh	-new
Ninnes	an ynys	-the island, isolated place
Noon, un, owen	an woen (goen)	-the downs
Ogo	ogo (gogo)	-cave
Owles	als	-cliff
Par, (parn)	porth	-cove, landing-place

8

Parc, park	park	-field, close
-parrett, parva, parvath	pervedh	-inner, middle
Pedn, pen, pe, p-	penn	-head, end, top
-pean	byghan	-little
Pit, pits	pytt, plural pyttys	-pit, pits
Pol, poll	poll (often for porth)	-pool
Pons, ponds, pols, pont	pons	-bridge
Porth, port, per, pr-, pol	porth	-cove, landing-place
Praze	pras	-meadow
-quin, -quidden	gwynn	-white
-quite	koes	-wood
Re, red, res, ris, ros, -rice	rys (often for ros)	-ford
Reen, -ridden, -ryn	run (slope), rynn (promontory), occasionally reden (bracken)	
Reeth	rydh (sometimes = rudh)	-free
Rose	ros (often for rys)	-heath, or promontory
Ruth	rudh	-red
Scawen, scow, -scoe	skawenn, plural skaw	-eldertree(s)
-sew, -sue	du	-black
Sparnon, spearn	spernenn, plural spern	-thorn
-stain	sten	-tin
Sten, Stephen, St	stumm	-bend
Tal, tol	tal	-brow,'next to'
Tol, toll	toll (often for tal)	-hole
Todden, ton, tane	tonn	-grassland
Towan	tewynn	-dune
Treath	treth	-beach, strand
Tre, trev, tor, tr-	tre	-farm, village
Trem, tren	tre'n (tre an)	-farm of the
Tres	ros (confused with rys)	-heath (or 'ford')
Ty	chi	-house
-va	va	-place
-vadden, -van	vann (bann)	-a height
Vear, veor	veur (meur)	-great
Vellan, vellyn, valley	velin (melin)	-mill
-vena, -venner	venydh (menydh)	-hill
Venton	fenten	-spring
-vose, voose	fos	-dyke
-vrane	vran (bran)	-crow (sometimes pers. name)
-vraze	vras (bras)	-big
-vrea, -vra	vre (bre)	-hill
Vounder	vownder (bownder)	-the cattle-track, lane
-warne	wern (gwern)	-alder trees, marsh
Wartha	wartha (gwartha)	-higher
-wen, -widden, -win, -wyn	wynn (gwynn)	-white
Wheal	hwel	-mine-working

-wins, -wint	wyns (gwyns)	-wind
-withen	wydhenn (gwydhenn)	-tree (but see main list)
-woolas	woeles (goeles)	-lower
-woon	oen (goen)	-downs
-zance	sans	-holy
Zawn	sawn	-cleft in cliffs

FIELDS AND MINES

The main list in this list book does not include many fieldnames, but, since many of these survive, often used for housing estates and also for the benefit of those looking at old records, here is a small sample.

Fieldnames:

Croft	kroft	-small holding
Dor, doar	dor	-ground, small plot
Erow, ali	erow	-acre
Gew, gue	gew (kew)	-close, usually near farm-house
Gweal	gwel	-open cultivated field
Lean	len	-strip or stitch
Park	park	-field or close
Praze	pras	-meadow
Vithan	vydhynn (budhynn)	-meadow

Most of these words may be followed by any of the descriptive elements in the above list, by the name of the owner, Croft Pascoe, Park Davey, etc., or by such phrases as these: (The word an is often omitted)

(an) Bannel	banal (banadhel)	-broom
Beath	bedh	-grave
Bowen	bewin	-beef
Bucca	boekka	-spirit, or (later) scarecrow
Chapel	chapel	-chapel
Dandrea	yn-dann an dre	-below the farm or town
(an) Darras	daras	-door
Dodnan	donnenn (tonnenn)	-piece of turf
Drain	dreyn	-thorns
Drea	dre (tre)	-home-field
Friglas	fordh eglos	-church-way
Grambla	grommlegh (krommlegh)	-cromlegh, stone monument
Grengy	greunji	-grange
Gwith	gwydh	-trees
Hor	hordh	-ram

Ithan (nathan)	*eythin*	-furze, gorse
Intranthewhenver	*yntra'n dhiw henfordh*	-between the two old roads
(an) Kine	*keyn*	-back, ridge
Mo	*mogh*	-pigs
Noath	*noeth*	-naked
Noonpoocas, onypokis	*an woen boekkyas*	-downs of the ghosts or spirits
Pan esse	*panes*	-parsnips
Peeth	*puth*	-well
Pillas	*pilas*	-a kind of oats, once staple diet
Skeber	*skiber*	-barn
Sowle	*sowl*	-stubble, thatch
Sperris	*spedhas*	-briars
Stenor	*stennor*	-tinner
Tarow	*tarow*	-bull
Tubman	*tommenn*	-hummock
Vaze	*a-ves*	-outer
Vor	*fordh*	-road
Vorn	*forn*	-furnace
Weeth	*woeth (goeth)*	-watercourse
Yeat	*yet*	-gate

The word konna (neck), used for narrow fields, also occurs in the common nickname Crackagodna (krakk y gonna), for very steep ones.

Mine Names:

A prospector's patch or 'bound' was christened in much the same way as a field. Actual mine-names usually begin with Wheal (hwel), a works, or Bal which usually means a larger conglomeration of mining setts. These names very often completed with the name of the land-owner, the 'adventurer' (entrepreneur) or their ladies. Because Wheal remained in fashion throughout the boom years of mining, many such names are half English, some deliberate puns like Wheal Prosper, Wheal Speed, or

Charles Dickens' Wheal Do'em', which accurately reflects the attitude of some adventurers to their investors. A few Cornish names recorded for mine-works, some of them very old, are listed below:

Crease an Pocket	*kres an poket*	-Middle of the pocket
Hagarowal	*hager awel*	-Foul Weather
Coffenoola	*koghenn ula*	-Open-work of the Owl
Wheal an Cleath (Clay)	*hwel an kleudh*	-Ditch Mine
Wheal an Howl	*h. an howl*	-Sun Mine
Wheal an Stearan	*h. an sterenn*	-The Star Mine
Wheal Mehal	*h. Mighal*	-(St) Michael's Mine
Wheal Maria, Variah	*h. Maria, Varia*	-Mary's Mine
Wheal Perran	*h. Perran*	-(St) Perran's Mine
Wheal 'Tis Gentle	*h. an dus jentyl*	-Gentleman's Mine

Naturally Wheal may be followed by any of the descriptive words or phrases in the above two lists – or of course many others.

A

Adjewednack	*Aswa wynsek*	-Gap + personal name
Aire	*Ardh*	-High place
Atarnun	*Alternon*	-St Non's altar
Amalveor, -widden	*Amal-veur, -wynn*	-Great (or white) edge
Anderton		-Under (lower) farm (Eng)
Andrewartha	*An dre-wartha*	-The higher farm
Angarrack Angarrick	*An garrek*	-The rock

Angear	An ger	-The fortified village
Angew	An gew	-The close
Angrowse	An grows	-The cross
Anhay	An hay	-The hedge or close
Anjarden	An jardin	-The garden
Anvoase	An fos	-The dyke
Ardevora (Veor)	Ardevrenn (Veur)	-The (great) farm on the watery land
Argal	Argel	-At the place of retreat
Asparagus Island		-(Eng.) (from wild plant)
August Rock	?Men Ogas	-possibly 'The near rock'
Ayr	Ardh	-High place

B

Bake		-(Eng.) 'Back', ridge
Baldhu	Bal du	-Black mine
Ball	Bal	-Mine
Balleswidden	Bal lys wynn	-The mine of (?)the white court
Banns	Bans	-High place
Barbican (Looe)	Barr byghan	-Little summit
Bareppa (see Berepper)		
Bargoes, Bargus	Bargoes	-Summit of the wood
Barncoose	Bronn an koes	-Wood hill
Barnoon	Barr'n woen	-Summit of the down(s)
Barrimaylor	Merther Maelor	-Burial-place of St Maylor
Barriper (see Berepper)		
Beara, berah		-Grove (Old English)
Benallack	Banadhlek	-Broombrake
Berepper		-Fine retreat (French) 'Beaurepere'
Berry		-Old hill-fort (Eng.)
Biggal	Begel	-Hummock
Bissoe	Besow	-Birch-trees
Blisland		-Celtic word + (Eng) land
Blowing-house		-From old tin foundry (Eng.)

Place names beginning BO, BOD, BOS, BE, etc., (also CAR, TRE and LAN) are often completed with name of the founder of the settlement.

These names are quite unfamiliar to us today. They resemble the names of characters in Old Welsh legend and history and are derived from names like Caratacus, current in Britain before the Romans came. Often we can not be certain about them for they may occur only once, but just a few can be found in their original form amongst the names of slaves, whose manumissions were recorded in the 10th century in the 'Bodmin Gospels'.

Below are a few' BOS' names where the second element is definitely a corrupt form of the founder's name:

Bejowan	*Dwelling of*	Ewein
Boconnoc		Conoc
Bodbrane		Bran
Bodiggo		Uuithgi (Gwithgy)
Bodilly		Ili
Bodithiel		Iudhael
Bodrigan		Rigan
Bogee, Bojea		Yuf
Bokenna		Ceneu
Bolenna,		-now
Bolitho		
Bollowal		? Lewhael
Boskennal		Cenwal
Bosmawgan		Maelcun
Bosworgey		Uuorci (Gorgy) or of UUithgi
Bosworlas		Gorloes
Bottallack		Taloc
Botternell, Boturnal		
Bodinnick	*Bos-dinek*	-Fortified dwelling, or else the second part may be a personal name, as, definitely, at St Tudy.
Bodmin	*Bos-venegh*	-Originally 'dwelling of the sanctuary,' later, 'of monks'.
Bodwen	*Bos-wynn*	-White dwelling
Bolankan		-?Possibly dwelling by defile
Bolingey	*Melinji*	-Mill house
Bollogas	*Bos-logos*	-Dwelling of mice (or personal name)
Bolventor		-Bold Venture (Eng. field-name)
Bonallack	*Banadhlek*	-Broombrake
Bonyalva	*Banadhelva*	-Broom place
Borlase (-Vath)	*Burlas (Vargh)*	-Probably 'Green bank '(of Mark)
Boscarn, Boscarne	*Bos-karn*	-Dwelling by rock pile
Boscastle		-Botterels castle (Eng.)
Boscawen	*?Bos-skawenn*	-Dwelling of eldertree (or Gawen's dwelling)
Boscean	*Bos-syghan*	-Dwelling at dry spot
Boscreege	*Bos-krug*	-Dwelling by mound or barrow
Bosence, Bosent	*Bos-sens*	-Dwelling of saints

14

Bosporthennis	*Bos-porth-ynys*	-Dwelling at the entrance to the isolated place
Bostrase, Bostraze	*Bos-stras*	-Dwelling in low ground
Boswedden	*Bos-wynn*	- -White dwelling
Boswin, Boswyn	*Bos-wynn*	-White dwelling
Botus fleming	*Bos-flumyes*	-Dwelling + obscure personal name
Bowdah		-Bend of wood (old English)
Bowden		-Curved hill (Eng)
Bozion	*Bronn-syghan*	-Breast of hill of dry spot
Bray	*Bre*	-Hill
Brea (Vean)	*Bre (vyghan)*	-(Little) hill
Breage		-Name of parish saint
Brendon		-Burnt hill (Eng.)
Brighton		-prob. Eng. 'Bright farm'
Brightor		-prob. Eng. 'Bright hill'
Browngelly	*Brenn-gelow*	-Hill + unknown word
Brown willy	*Bronn-wynnlegh*	-Hill of white flat stone probably not 'wenyli' -of swallows)
Brynn	*Brenn*	-Hill
Budock	*Budhek*	-Name of Saint
Burlorne	*Bos-elowenn*	-Dwelling of elmtree
Burncoose	*Bronn-an-koes*	-Hill or top of wood
Burngullow	*Brenn-golow*	-Bright hill ('hill of light')
Burniere	*Brynn-hir*	-Long hill
Burras	*Berr-rys*	-Short ford
Burraton		-Eng. 'Boar' or 'hill' town
Bury		-Eng. Old hill-fort

C

Cadgwith	*Kaswydh*	-Bushes (poss. Personal name)
Cadsonbury		-Hill-fort at Cadoc's farm (Eng.)
Cadythew	*Karrek dhu*	-Black rock
Caer Bran	*Ker-vran*	-Fortified village of Bran (pers. name)
Cairo	*Keryow*	-Fortified villages
Calamansak		-poss. 'Retreat on small mound'
Calenick	*Kelynnek*	-Holly-bushes
Callenowth	*Kelli-gnowek*	-Nut grove
Camborne	*Kammbronn*	-Curve of the hill
Camelford		-Probably 'Curved Estuary' + Eng. Ford.

15

Canakey	*Karn an Ki*	-Rock-pile of the dog
Canaglaze	*Karn-glas*	-Blue-green rock-pile
Cannalidgey	*Kanol Isy*	-Middle (of parish) of Issey
Caragloose	*Karrek Loes*	-Grey Rock
Carbis	*Karrbons*	-Cart-bridge
Carciaze	*Krug-glas*	-Blue mound or burrow
Cardew	*Ker-dhu*	-Black hill-fort
Cardinham	*Ker-dhinan*	-Hill-fort or Dinan (pers. name)
Cargenwen	*Ker-Geynwynn*	-Hill-fort of Keynwynn
Cargreen	*Karrek-reun*	-Seal rock
Carleen, Carleon	*Ker-leghyon*	-Hill fort of flat stones
Carlidnack, Carlinick		-Hill-fort & personal name
Carloggas	*Ker-logos*	-Hill-fort of mice (or else pers. name)
Carn, Carne	*Karn*	-Rock-pile
Carnaquidden	*Kernek-wynn*	-White rock-pile (or nook)
Carnbargus	*Karn Bargos*	-'Carn' (rock pile) of kite
Carn Base	*Karn Bas*	-Shallow carn
Carn Boel	*Karn Moel*	-Bald, bare carn
Carn, Clew, Clough	*Karn Klog*	-possible 'Crag carn'
Carn Du	*Karn Du*	-Black carn
Carnewas	*Karn-havos*	-Carn of summer pasture
Carnglaze	*Karn-glas*	-Blue-green rock-pile
Carnglooze	*Karrek-loes*	-Grey rock
Carn Haut, Hot	*Karn hatt*	-Hat-shaped carn
Carnkie	*Karn Ki*	-Dog carn
Carnmarth	*Karn Margh*	-Mark's carn
Cammenellis	*Karn-menelys*	-Rocks piled like sheaves
Carnon		-Poss. Small Carn
Carnsew	*Karn-du*	-Black carn
Carnsmerry	*Karn-ros-meur*	-Carn of the great heath
Carnyorth	*Karn-yorgh*	-Roebuck carn or rockpile
Carrack Gladden	*Karrek-lann*	-Rock on the bank
Carracks (The)	*Karregi*	-The rocks(Eng. plural)
Carrag-a-pilez	*Karrek-an-pilas*	-The rock of oats (pillas)
Carrick Du	*Karrek Dhu*	-Black Rock
Carrick Luz	*Karrek Loes*	-Grey rock
Carrick Nath	*Karrek Nadh*	-Hewn rock
Carrick Roads		-Roadstead or achorage of the rock
Carthew	*Ker-dhu*	-Black hill-fort
Cartuther	*Krug Tudher*	-Teudar's mound or barrow
Carvannel	*Ker-vanadhel*	-Hill-fort of broom
Carvean	*Ker-vyghan*	-Little hill-fort
Carveddras	*Ker-Vedras*	-Hill-fort of Modred (pers. name)

Carvinack		-Stony hill-fort or Gwinoc's fort
Carwen	*Ker-wynn*	-White, or Gwyn's hill-fort
Carworgie		-Hill-fort of Gorgi
Carwythenack		-Hill-fort of Gwethenoc
Castle-an-Dinas	*Kastell-an-dinas*	-Castle (a duplicated name since 'an dynas' means 'the fort')
Castle Canyke	*Kastell Kenek*	-Conoc's castle
Castle Dore	*? Kastell Dour*	-Perhaps 'severe castle'
Castle Gotha	*Kastell Goedhow*	-possibly 'Geese Castle'
Castle Wary		-poss. 'Castle of the playing-place'(gwari)
Catchfrench		-Free hunting (French) 'Chasse-franche'
Chacewater	*(Dowr an chas)*	-(Eng.) stream In hunting-ground
Chapel Amble	*Chapel Amal*	-Chapel on the border.
Charlestown		-named from its builder, Charles Rashleigh. Its old name was Porth (or Poll) Mur -Great Cove
Chenall, Chenhale	*Chi an hal*	-House on the moor
Chenhalls	*Chi an als*	-House on the cliff
Chenoweth	*Chi nowydh*	-New House
Chipponds	*Chi-pons*	-Bridge House
Chiverton	*Chi war'n tonn*	-House on the grassland
Choon, Choone	*Chi-woen*	-House on the downs
Chun	*Chi-woen*	-House on the downs
Chyandour	*Chi an dowr*	-House of the water or stream
Chyanvounder	*Chi an vownder*	-House of the lane
Chybucca	*Chiboekka*	-Ghost or spirit house
Chycarne(e)	*Chikarn*	-Carn (rock pile) house
Chycoose	*Chikoes*	-Wood house
Chygwidden		-House of Uuorguin
Chyngwith	*Chi an gwydh*	-House of the trees
Chykembro	*Chi Kembro*	-House of Welshman
Chynhale	*Chi'n hal*	-House on the moor
Chynoweth	*Chi nowydh*	-New house
-pons	*-pons*	-Bridge house
-praze	*-pras*	-Meadow house
-reen	*-run*	-Hillside house
-rose	*-ros*	-Heath house
Chysauster	*Chi-Sylvester*	-Silvester's house
Chytan	*Chi war'n tonn*	-House on the grassland
-todden	*Chi'n tonn*	-House on the grassland

Chyvarton	Chi war'n tonn	-House on the grassland
Chywoon(e)	Chi-woen	-Downs house
Cleave		-Cliff (Eng.)
Clennick, Clinnick	Kelynnek	-Hollybushes
Clodgy	Klavji	-Leper-house
Coldharbour		-(Eng.) Field-name
Coldrennick, Coldrinnick	Kildreynek	-Thorny nook
Coldvreath	Kelli-vrith	-Speckled grove
Coldquite	Kil-koes	-Back of the wood
Colvannick		-?Prominent hill
Colvennor	Kil-venydh	-Back of the hill
Come-to-good		-(Eng.) Probably nickname for field
Comfort		-?(Eng.)? Coombe, 'valley', ford
Cornprigney	Gwel Kloghprennyer	-Gallowtrees field
Condurrow		-Poss. Junction of waters
Connor Downs		-Poss. from Old Irish word for 'harbour'
Coosebean	Koes byghan	-Little wood
Coosewartha	Koes-wartha	-Upper wood
Costislost		-Eng.-Nickname for poor field
Cornakee, Cornakey	Karn an Ki	-Carn or rock pile of the dog
Cowyjack		-Hollowed out place
Crane	Ker-vran	-Hillfort of Bran (pers. name) or crow
Crankan		-Hillfort & personal name
Creak-a-vose	Krug an fos	-Mound or barrow of the dyke
Creegbrawse	Krug bras	-Great mound or barrow
Cregoe	Krugow	-Barrows or mounds
Cribba	Kribow	-Crests
Crift		-Croft, small-holding
Crigmurrian	Krug-Meryan	-Merien's mound or barrow
Croft an Creeg	Kroft an krug	-Croft (small holding) of the barrow
Croft an Growse	Kroft an grows	-of the cross
Croft Michael	Kroft Mighal	-Michael's croft
Croft Noweth	Kroft nowydh	-New croft
Croft Pascoe	Kroft Pasko	-Pascoe's croft
Croftow	Kroftow	-Crofts
Crowgey	Krowji	-Cottage, hovel
Crows-an-wra	Krows an wragh	-Witch's cross
Crugmeer	Krug-meur	-Great mound or barrow
Crugoes	Krugow	-Barrows, mounds (Eng. plurals' added)
Crumplehorn	Tremaelhorn	-Maelhorn's farm
Cubert	Kubert	-Saints name

Culdrose	*Kil-ros*	-possible 'nook in the heath'
Cury		-from Corentyn, the parish priest
Cutcare	*Koes-ker*	-Wood of hill-fort
Cutcrew	*Koes-know*	-Nut wood
Cutmadock	*Koes-Madek*	-Madoc's wood
Cutmere	*Koes-meur*	-Great wood
Cutparrett	*Koes-pervedh*	-Inner or middle wood

D

Dannon	*Dew-nans*	-Two valleys
Darracott		-(Eng.) Dodda's farm
Degibna		-From chapel of St Degiman
Delabole		-From 'Delyow', stream or district name
Demeiza	*Din-Melsa*	-Fort of Maeldaf
Dennis	*Dinas*	-Fort
Denzel		-Probably: Fort ('din') & personal name
Devoral	*Deverel*	-Watery place
Devoran	*Devren*	-Wet valley
Dewey		-Common stream name (? 'Goddess')
Dinas	*Dinas*	-Fort
Dizzard	*Deserth*	-Very steep (place)
Dobwalls		-probably corrupt form of Doublebois
Dolcoath	*Dor koth*	-probably 'Old field'
Dollar Ogo		-Dollar Cave (Eng. order)
Domellick	*Din Maeloc*	-Maeloc's fort
Dorminack	*Dor-meynek*	-Stony ground
Dosmary Pool		-'-mary' is probably 'mere' (Eng.)
Doublebois	*(Dew goes)*	-Two woods (French)
Dowgas	*Dew-goes*	-Two woods
Downderry		-Probably Eng. meaning obscure
Dowran	*Dowran*	-Watering Place
Draynes	*Dreynys*	-Thorny place
Drewollas	*An Dre-woeles*	-The lower farm
Drift	*An Drev*	-The farm
Drym	*Drumm*	-Ridge
Duloe	*Dew logh*	-Between the two (river) Looe(s)
Dunheved		-(Eng.) Down-head, head of downs

Dunmere	*Din meur*	-Great fort
Dupath		-Probably Eng. 'Thieves' path
Duporth	*Dew borth*	-(Farm of the) two coves

E

Eglaroose	*Eglos-ros*	-Church on heath or promontary
Egloshayle	*Eglos-heyl*	-Church on estuary
-kerry	*Keri*	-Church of St Kerry
-merther	*-merther*	-Church of burial place of saint
-rose	*-ros*	-Church on heath or promontory
Engelley	*An Gelli*	-The grove
Engollen	*An gollenn*	-The hazeltree
Ennis-vath	*Ynys-Vargh*	-Mark's part of isolated land
Ennis-worgey	*Ynys-Worgi*	-Gorgi's part of isolated land

F

Fentengoe	*Fenten-gog*	-Cuckoo's spring
Fentervean	*Fenten-vyghan*	-Little spring
Fentengollen	*Fenten-gollenn*	-Spring of hazle-tree (or of Kolan)
Fentongoose	*Fenten-goes*	-Spring of the wood
Feock	*Lannfek*	-From parish saint
Fowey	*Fow-wydh*	-Beechtrees' (name of river)
Fraddon	*Frodan*	-Small stream
Fursnewth	*Fos-nowydh*	-New dyke

G

Gabbons		-Probably from 'kamm'-crooked
Gare	*An ger*	-Hill-fort
Garras	*Garow-ros*	-Rough heath
Gaverigan	*Gover-gwynn*	-White stream
Gazick	*An gasek*	-The mare
Gear	*An ger*	-Hill-fort
Geevor	*An gowfordh*	-Sunken road
Gelly	*An gelli*	-Grove
Germoe	*Germogh*	-Name of parish priest
Gerrans	*Gerens*	-Name of Cornish king and saint Gerent
Gew (Graze)	*An Gew (Gres)*	-(Middle) close field
Gillian	*An gilenn*	-Nook or creek

Gilley, Gilly (vean)	*An gelli (vyghan)*	-(Little) grove
Gilley, Gilly (wartha)	*An gelli (wartha)*	-(Higher) grove
Gloweth	*Glow-wydh*	-probably: Charcoal wood
Gluvian		-Name of parish saint
Godolphin	*Godolghynn*	-(possibly) Little mound
Goenrounsen	*Goen-ronsyn*	-(possibly) Downs of the nag
Golant	*Goelnans (or Gwelnans)*	-Feast or field of the valley
Goldsithney	*Goel-Sythni*	-Feast of Sithney
Goonamarth	*Goen an margh*	-Downs of the horse
Goon Bell	*Goen Bell*	-Far downs
-goose	*-goes*	-Wood downs
-gumpus	*-gompes*	-Level downs
-havern	*-havar*	-Downs with summer fallowland
-hilly		-Briny (possibly 'hunting') downs
-hingey	*-henji*	-Downs of the old house
-hoskyn		-Hoskyn's downs
-laze	*-las*	-blue-green downs
-vean	*-vyghan*	-Little downs
-vrea	*-vre*	-Hill downs
Gormellick	*Goen-Maelioc*	-Downs of Maelloc (pers. name)
Gorrangorras	*Goen-an-gores*	-Downs of the weir
Goss Moor	*An gors*	-Marsh & Eng. moor
Govarrow	*Goverow*	-Streams
Grampound	*Pons-meur*	-French 'Grand Pont '. Both names mean Great Bridge
Gratna		-Eng. for rough field
Greensplatt		-Eng. dialect for 'green place'
Greeb	*An Grib*	-Crest
Gregwartha	*An Grug-wartha*	-Higher barrow or mound
Gribba, Gribben	*An Gribenn*	-Small crest
Gue Graze	*Gew Gres*	-Middle close, field
Gullaveis	*Gwel-a-ves*	-Far field

Gunnislake		-Probably: Eng. 'Gonna's stream or possibly connected with 'Gunnis' a worked out part of a mine
Gunvena	*Gwynnvenydh*	-White hill
Gwarder	*Gwyr'dhowr*	-probably Green water
Gwarnick	*Gwernek*	-Alder-grove or marsh
Gwarth—an-drea	*Gwartha an dre*	-Top of the town
Gwavas	*Gwavos*	-Winter farm

Gwealavellan	*Gwel-an-velin*	-Open field of the mill
-dues	*-du*	-Black field (Eng. plural 's', added)
-hellis	*-Hellys*	-Helston field
-mayowe		-Mayowe's field
-mellin	*-melin*	-Open field of the mill
Gwendra	*Gwynndre*	-White field
Gwendreath	*Gwynndreth*	-White beach
Gwennap	*Lannwenep*	-Name of parish saint
Gwinear		-Name of parish saint
Gwithian		-Name of parish saint
Gyllyngdune	*An gilenn dhown*	-Deep nook or bay
Gyllyngvase	*An gilenn vas*	-Shallow nook or bay

H

Halabezack	*Hal-wibesek*	-Moor of gnats
Halamanning	*Hal-amanenn*	-Butter moor
Hallaze	*Hal-las*	-Green moor
Hallow	*Halow*	-Moors
Halsferran	*Als-Ifarn*	-Hell cliff
Halvana	*Hir-venydh*	-Long hill
Halviggan	*?Hal-vyghan*	-(possibly) Small moor
Halwin, Halwyn	*Hal-wynn*	-White moor
Halzaphron	*Als-Ifarn*	-Hell cliff
Harlyn	*Hir-lynn*	-Long lake
Harris, Harros	*Hir-ros*	-Long heath
Harvose	*Hir-fos*	-Long dyke.
Hay	*Hay*	-Hedge or field
Hayle	*Heyl*	-Estuary
Hea	*Hay*	-Hedge or field
Hele		-(Eng.) Nook or angle
Heligan	*Heligenn*	-Willowtree
Helland	*Hen-lann*	-Old holy place
Hellangove	*Hel-an-gov*	-Hall of the smith
Hellesveor	*Hellys-veur*	-Great 'Oldcourt'
Helligan	*Heligenn*	-Willowtree
Helsbury	*Hellys*	-'Old Court' & (Eng.) for hill fort
Helston	*Hellys*	-'Old Court' & (Eng.) 'town'
Hendra	*Hendre*	-Old farm
Henforth	*Henfordh*	-Old road
Hengar	*Henger*	-Old hill-fort
Hennett	*Heudh-nans*	-Happy valley
Henver	*Henfordh*	-Old road
Hernis	*Hirnans*	-Long valley

22

Herodsfoot	Hir-arth	-Long yard & (Eng.) 'valley bottom'
Hessenford		-(Eng.) possibly 'Hag's ford'
Hewas	Havos	-Summer pasture
Hole	?Hal	-Moor or (Eng.) hallow
Hor Point	Penn-hordh	-Ram Point
Huthnance	Heudh-nans	-Happy valley

I

Illiswilgig	Ynys-welsek	-Grassy island
Illogan		-Name of parish saint
Ince	Ynys	-Island, isolated place
Indian Queens		-(Eng.) probably from inn sign
Irish	Arys	-Stubble

J

Joppa	An Shoppa	-Shop, blacksmith's shop

K

Karslake		-(Eng.) Cress-pool or stream
Keigwin	Ke-gwynn	-White hedge
Kellivose	Kelli-fos	-Grove of the dyke
Kellow	Kelliow	-Groves
Kelly (Bray)	Kelli (Bre)	-Grove (of the hill)
Kelynack	Kelynnek	-Hollybushes
Kenegie	Keunegi	-Reed-bed, marshes
Kenidjack	Keunysek	-Place for gathering firewood
Kennegie, Kennegy	Keunegi	-Reed-bed, marshes
Kenwyn		-Name of parish saint
Kernick	Kernik	-Nook or corner
Kerrow	Keryow	-Camps, hill-forts
Kerslake		-Cress pool, stream (Eng.)
Kestle	Kastell	-Castle or village
Kilcobben	Kil-kromm	-Crooked nook (Probably)
Killatown	Kelliow	-'Groves' & Eng. 'town' or 'farm'
Killiganogue	Kelli-gnowek	-?Nut-bearing grove
Killigerran	Kil-Gerens	-Retreat of Gerrans (St and King)
Killigrew	Kelli-gnow	-Nut grove
Killiow	Kelliow	-Groves
Kilmarth, Kilmar	Kil-Margh	-Retreat of Mark (or possibly 'horse')
Kynance	Kownans	-Ravine

L

Laddenvean	An-Lann-vyghan	-Little bank
Ladock	Lasek	-Name of parish saint
Laity	Leti	-Dairy ('milk-house')
Lamellion	Nans-melin	-Mill valley
Lamellyn, Lamellyon	Nans-melin	-Mill valley
Lanarth	Lannergh	-Clearing
Lancarrow	Nans-karow	-Stag valley
Lands End	Penn-an-wlas	-(Cornish with same meaning)
Landewednack	Lannsewynek	-Holy enclosure of St Gwinwallo
Landlooe	Nans-Logh	-Valley of River Looe
Landreyne	Nans-dreyn	-Valley of thorns
Landrine	Nans-dreyn	-Valley of thorns
Laneast		-Holy place + personal name
Langdon		-Long hill(Eng)
Langford		-Long ford (Eng)
Lanhay	An hay	-The hedge (with both French & Cornish words for 'the')
Lanherne	Lann-Hernow	-Holy place of St Hernow
Lanhydrock	Lannhedrek	-Holy place of Hidroc
Lankelly	Nans-kelli	-Valley of grove
Lanner	Lannergh	-Clearing
Lanseague	Nans-teg	-Fair valley
Lanseaton	Nans-seythyn	-Valley of winding stream
Lanteague	Nans-teg	-Fair valley
Lanteglos	Nans-eglos	-Church valley
Lantinning		-Holy place of St Yntennyn
Lantewey	Nans-Dewy	-Valley of River Dewy
Lanyon	Lynn-yeyn	-Cold pool
Launceston	Lann-Stefan	-Holy place of St Stephen + (Eng.) town
Leah	Legh	-Flat stone
Lee, Ley	Legh	-Flat stone (or Eng. 'lay field')
Lel ant	Lann-Anta	-Holy place of St Anta
Leskernick		-?Rocky ford
Lesnewth	Lys-nowydh	-New court
Lesquite	Lost-koes	-'Tail of the wood'
Lestoon	Lost-woen	-'Tail of the downs'
Lestowder	Lys-Teudar	-Court of (King) Teudar
Lewannick		-Holy place + personal name
Lewarne		-Holy place or valley of eldertrees
Lidcott, Lidcutt	Loes-koes	-Grey wood
Linkinhorne	Lannkenhorn	-Holy place of St Kenhorn (stressed on 'horn')

Liskeard	*Lyskerrys*	-Court + personal name
Little Petherick	*Nans-fenten*	-Petherick is a late form of St Petroc, (Cornish means 'valley with spring')
Lizard	*Lys-ardh*	-possibly 'High court'
Loe	*Logh*	-Sea-lake, estuary
Looe	*Logh*	-Sea-lake, estuary
Lostwithiel	*Lostwydhyel*	-Tail of wooded land
Ludcott	*Loes-koes*	-Grey wood
Ludgvan	*Lusuan*	-Unknown, first part may be 'grey'
Luxulyan	*Log-Sulyen*	-Cell, or holy place, of St Sulyan
Lydcott	*Loes-koes*	-Grey wood

M

Mabe	*Lann-Vab*	-Name of parish saint
Maders	*Medhros*	-Middle of heath
Maen Du	*Men du*	-Black stone
Maen Lay	*Men legh*	-Flat Stone
Maen Porth	*Men porth*	-Stone of the cove
Magor	*Magor*	-Old walls, ruins
Maker	*Magor*	-Old walls, ruins
Manaccan	*Managhan*	-Minster
Marazanvose	*Marghas an Fos*	-Market of the dyke
Marazion	*Marghas-vyghan*	-Little market
Marketjew	*Marghas Dy Yow*	-Thursday market (Both Marazion and Marketjew came to mean the same settlement)
Mawgan		-Name of parish saint
Mawnan		-Name of parish saint
Meadrose	*Medhros*	-Middle of heath
Mean Mellin	*Men melin*	-Millstone

Mean Toll	*Men an Toll*	-Holed stone
Medrose	*Medhros*	-Middle of heath
Mehal Mill	*Melin Vighal*	-Michael's mill
Mellan-coose	*Melin-goes*	-Mill in the wood
Mellan-noweth	*Melin-nowydh*	-New mill
Mellan-vrane	*Melin-vran*	-Crow mill or mill of Bran (pers name)
Mellingey	*Melinji*	-Mill house
Mellingoose	*Melin-goes*	-Wood mill (ie. 'in the wood')
Menaclidgey	*Menydh-kloesow*	-Hill of hurdles
Menacrin	*Menydh-krin*	-Dry hill
Menadarva	*Merther Derva*	-Burial place of St Derva
Mena-dew(s)	*Menydh du*	-Black hill (sometimes with Eng. plural)
Mena-glaze	*Menydh glas*	-Blue green hill
Mena-gwins	*Menydh gwyns*	-Windy hill
Men an Tol	*Men an Toll*	-Stone with the hole
Men Aver	*Men an Aver*	-The goat stone
Menear	*Men-hir*	-Long stone (from monument)
Menerdue	*Menydh-du*	-Black hill
Menhay	*Meneghi*	-Sanctuary (religious)
Menheniot	*Mahenyet*	-possibly Place (or sanctuary) of St Neot
Menherion	*Meyn-hiryon*	-Longstones (monument)
Menhyr	*Men-hir*	-Long stone (monument)
Menkee	*Men-ki*	-Dog stone
Mennergwidden	*Menydh-gwynn*	-White hill
Mennaridden	*Menydh-reden*	-Hill of ferns
Men Par	*Men porth*	-Cove stone
Menwinnion	*Meyn-wynnyon*	-White or blessed stones
Men-y-grib	*Men-an-grib*	-Stone of the crest
Merrose	*Medhros*	-Middle of the heath
Merther	*Merther*	-Burial place of saint (from 'Martyr')
Mesmear	*Mes-meur*	-Great field
Metherell		-Middle hill (Eng.)
Methrose	*Medhros*	-Middle of the heath
Mevagissey	*Meva hag Ysi*	-'Meva and Issey', the parish saints
Minack	*Meynek*	-Stony (field)
Minear	*Men-hir*	-Longstone (monument)
Mingoose	*Min-koes*	-Edge of the wood
Molevenny	*Moel-venydh*	-Bare hill
Molingey	*Melinji*	-Mill house
Molinnis	*Moel-ynys*	-Bare island or isolated place
Mongleath	*Mengleudh*	-Quarry or mine

Morvah	*Morvath*	-probably name of original parish saint
Mouls	*Mols*	-Wether sheep
Mousehole	*Porth-ynys*	-Eng. (Cornish means 'Island Cove')
Mulfra, Mulvra	*Moelvre*	-Bare hill
Mylor		-Name of parish saint

N

Nancarrow	*Nans-karow*	-Stag valley
Nance	*Nans*	-Valley
Nancegollan	*Nans-igollenn*	-Valley of the whet-stone
Nance-loe	*Nans-logh*	-Sea-lake valley
Nance-mere	*Nans-meur*	-Great valley
Nance-trisack	*Nans-dreysek*	-Brambly valley
Nance-vallon	*Nans-avalenn*	-Appletree valley
Nance-wrath	*Nans-an-wragh*	-Witch's valley
Nankelly, Nankilly	*Nans-kelli*	-Grove valley
Nanpean	*Nans-byghan*	-Little valley
Nanscawen	*Nans-skawenn*	-Eldertree valley
Nanscow	*Nans-skaw*	-Valley of eldertrees
Nansloe	*Nans-logh*	-Valley of sea-lake
-ladron	*Nans-ladron*	-Valley of thieves (may be corrupted from Lanhadron 'holy place of St. Hadron)
-mellyn	*Nans-melin*	-Mill valley
Nanteague	*Nans-teg*	-Fair valley
Nantrisack	*Nans-dreysek*	-Brambly valley
Nare	*An ardh*	-The height
Newquay	*Tewynn Porth Lestri*	-(Eng.) Cornish = 'Sand dune by ships cove' A reading of an old name for the place which has been used for some years.
Ninnes, Ninnis	*An Ynys*	-The island or isolated place
Noon Billas	*An-woen-bilas*	-The downs of oats

O

Ogo Dour	*Ogo-dowr*	-Water Cave
Ogo Pons	*Ogo-pons*	-Bridge cave

P

Padjagarrack	*Peder-karrek*	-Four rocks
Padstow	*Lannwedhenek*	-Holy place of St Petroc (Eng.) The Cornish 'Lann' was dedicated to another saint, Guethenoc.
Panters Bridge	*? Pons Ihesu*	-If correctly identified, this was 'Jesus Bridge'
Par (Bean)	*Porth (Byghan)*	-(Little) cove
Parc-an-als	*Park-an-als*	-Field of the cliff
an Growes	*-an-grows*	-Field of cross
Bean	*Byghan*	-Little field
Caragloose	*Karrek-loes*	-Field of the grey rock
Eglos	*-eglos*	-Church field
an Creet	*-an-krug*	-Field of the mound or barrow
Park an Bowen	*Park-an-bewin*	-Beef field
an Castle	*-an-kastell*	-Castle field
an Gear	*-an-ger*	-Hill-fort field
an Fold	*-an-fold*	-Field of the sheepfold
an Tidnoe	*-an-fentynyow*	-Field of the springs
Brauze	*-bras*	-Big field
Parkendillick	*Park-an-deylek*	-Field of the dung-heap
-en Gear	*-an-ger*	-Field of the hill-fort
-en Gew	*-an-gew*	-Field of the enclosure
Hoskyn		-Hoskyn's field
Uren		-Uren's Field
Venton	*an-fenten*	-Field of the spring
Parnvoose	*Porth-an-fos*	-Cove of the dyke
Pednandrea	*Penn-an-dre*	-End of the town
Pednanvounder	*-an-vownder*	-End of the lane or cattle-track
Pedn Brose	*-bras*	-Big headland
Pedn Men Du	*-men-du*	-Headland of black stone
Pedn Myin	*-meyn*	-End of the stones
-vadan	*-tal-vann*	-Headland by the height
-y-ke	*-an-ke*	-End of the hedge
Penlean, Penlyn	*Pennlynn*	-End of the lake
Pelynt	*Plyw-Nynt*	-Parish. of (Saint) Nent. or Non

Penadlake, Penadlick	*Banadhlek*	-Broom-brake
Pen-a-gader	*Penn-an-gador*	-Headland of the chair
Penair	*Penn-ardh*	-End of the heights
Pen-a-maen	*Penn-an-men*	-End of the stone or stones
-bothidna	*-budhynnyow*	-End of the meadows
-bugle	*-bugel*	-Shepherds hill
-calenick	*-kelynnek*	-End of hollybush grove
-carrow	*-karow*	-Hill of the stag
-coose	*-koes*	-End of the wood
-corse	*-kors*	-End of the marsh
-deen	*-din*	-Headland with fort
-dennis	*-dinas*	-Headland with fort
Pendoggett	*Penn-dew-goes*	-End of the two woods
-dour	*-dowr*	-End of the water or stream
-dower	*-dowr*	-End of the water or stream
-drea	*-an-dre*	-End of town
-enys	*-an-ynys*	-End of the island
-gelly	*-an-gelli*	-End of the grove
-gersick	*-an-gersek*	
	(a variation of *an-gorsek*)	
		-End of the reedbed, marsh
-gilly	*-an-gelli*	-End of the grove
-glaze	*-glas*	-Blue-green head
-gover	*-gover*	-End of the stream
-hale	*-hal*	-End of the moor
-hallow	*-halow*	-End of the moors
-halt	*-als*	-End of the cliff
Penhalvean, (-vear)	*Penn-hal-vyghan (-veur)*	
		-(Great) or little 'End of the moor'
-helllck	*-helik*	-End of the willow trees
-hole	*-hal*	-End of the moor
-kelly	*-kelli*	-End of the grove
-kestle	*-kestell (*a variation of *kastell*)	
		-End of the castle or village
-lee	*-legh*	-Headland of flat stones
-menor	*-menydh*	-End of hill
-nance, -nans	*-nans*	-End of valley
-nant	*-nans*	-End of valley
-nare	*-an-ardh*	-End of the heights
-olva -olver	*-an-woelva*	-End of the lookout
Pennycomequick		-(Eng.) nickname for good field
Pennytinney	*Penn-fentynyow*	-End of the springs
Penpoll	*Penn-poll*	-End of pool
-ponds	*-pons*	-End of the bridge
-pont	*-pons*	-End of the bridge

-praze	*-pras*	-End of the meadow
-quite	*-koes*	-End of the wood
-ryn	*-rynn*	-End of the slope
-rose	*-ros*	-End of the heath or promontory
Pentevale	*Penn-fenten-Fala*	-Source (spnnghead) of River Fal
Penstraze	*Penn-stras*	-End of the valley bottom
Pentire (Glaze)	*Penntir-glas*	-(Blue-green) Headland
Pentreath	*Penntreth*	-End of the beach
Penventon	*Penn-fenten*	-head of the spring (source)
-ventinue	*-fentynyow*	-Springheads
-vose	*-fos*	-End of dyke
-warne	*-an-wern*	-End of eldertrees or marsh
Penwith	*Pennwydh*	-Extremity, end
Penydevern	*Penn-an-dowran*	-End or head of the wet valley
Penzance	*Penn-sans*	-Holy head
Percuil	*Porth-kul*	-probably 'Narrow cove
Perranarworthal	*Peran-ar-wydhel*	-Combination of two placenames one name after St Perran, the other possibly meaning 'On the thicket'
Perranuthnoe		-from Saints Peran and Guethenoc
Perranzabuloe	*Pyran-treth*	-Perran (name of saint) in the sand: (Lat) Cornish name identical in meaning
Petherwin		-Blessed Saint Padarn (parish saint)
Pigeon Ogo		-(Eng.) Pigeon + cave
Pill		-(Eng.) 'creek'
Pits Mingle	*Pyttys Mengleudh*	-Quarry pits
Place	*Plas*	-Large house
Polangrain	*Poll-an-growynn (or greun)*	
		-Pool of the gravel (or 'grain')
Poldew-dhu,-du	*Poll-du*	-Black pool
-gazick	*-an-gasek*	-Mare's pool
-glase, -glaze	*-glas*	-Blue-green pool
-gooth	*-goedh*	-Goose pool
-gover	*-gover*	-Pool or end of stream
Pol -grain, -grean, -green	*-growynn*	-Gravel pool
-hendra	*-hendra*	-Pool of the old farm
-higey	*-heyji*	-Pool of the ducks
-kanoggo, -kanuggo	*-kroenogow*	-Pool of toads
-kernogo	*-kroenogow*	-Pool of toads
-kinghorne	*-Kenhorn*	-Pool of Kenhorn (personal name stressed on 'horne')

Pollaughan	*Poll-oghen*	-Ox pool
Polmarth	*Poll-margh*	-Horse pool or Marks pool
Pol-mear	*Poll-meur*	-Great pool
Polmennor	*Penn-menydh*	-End of hill
Polperro	*Porth-Pyra*	-Cove + probably pers. name
Polpry	*Poll-pri*	-Clay-pit
Polridmouth	*Porth-Redman*	-probably cove + pers. name
Polruan	*Porth-Ruan*	-Cove of Ruan (pers .;name)
Polscatha	*Porth-skathow*	-Boats cove
Polstain	*Poll-sten*	-Tin-pit -mine
Polstangey	*Pons-Tangy*	-Bridge of Tangey (pers. name)
Polstean, Polstein	*Poll-sten*	-Tin-pit mine
-strong	*-stronk*	-Dirty pool
-treworgey		-Treworgey Pool
-venten, -venton	*-fenten*	-Spring pool, or probably 'Springhead'
-whele	*-hwil*	-poss. Pool of beetles
-wrath	*-an-wragh*	-Witch's pool
Ponjou	*Ponsow*	-Bridges
Ponsandane	*Pons-an-den,* *Pons-an-deyn*	-Either 'the man's bridge' or 'The dean's bridge'
Ponsanooth	*Pons-an-woedh*	-Bridge of the goose
Ponsmain	*Pons-men*	-Stone bridge
Ponsmere	*Pons-meur*	-Great bridge
Ponsongath	*Pons-an-gath*	-Bridge of the cat
Ponsonjoppa	*Pons-an-joppa*	-Bridge of the smith's shop
Pont	*Pons*	-Bridge
Porn Boe	*Porth-an-bogh*	-Cove of the buck
Porthallow	*Porth-alow*	-Cove of Alaw (pers. name)
Porthbean	*Porth-byghan*	-Little cove
-curno	*-Kernow*	-Cove of Curno (pers. name)
Porth -glaze	*-glas*	-Blue-green cove
-gwarra		-Cove + personal name
-gwidden	*-gwynn*	-White cove
Porthkea	*Porth-Ke*	-Entrance to parish of St Kea
Porthledden	*Porth-ledan*	-Broad cove
-leven	*-Leven*	-Cove of St Levan (not 'leven' = calm)
-loe	*-logh*	-Cove of sea-lake
-mear, meor	*-meur*	-Great cove
-mellin	*-Melvan*	-Cove of St Melyan
-nanven	*-an-anwan*	-probably 'Anvil cove'
-pean	*-byghan*	-Little cove
-scatho	*-skathow*	-Cove of boats
-towan	*-tewynn*	-Cave of sand-dune
Porth Holland	*Porth-hen-lann*	-Cove of the old holy place

Port Isaac	-Yssak	-Cove + personal name
Loe, Looe	-Logh	-Cove of the sea-lake
Mellon	-melin	-Mill cove
Portreath	Porth-treth	-Cove on the beach
Port Quin	Porth-gwynn	-White cove
Praa (Prah)	Porth-an-wragh	-Witch or hag cove
Praze	Pras	-Meadow
-an-beeble	Pras-an-bibell	-Meadow of the? pipe
-gooth	-goedh	-Goose meadow
-ruth	-rudh	-Red meadow
Predannack (Wollas)	Penn-redenek (Woeles)	
		-(Lower) Headland of fern-brake
Pridden	Penn-rynn	-Head or end of hillside
Prideaux		-French 'By the water'
Probus	Lann-Broboes	-Name of saint

Q

Quethiock		-Name of saint (just possibly Cadoc)
Quillets		-Small fields (Eng. dialect)
Quintrell Downs		-from personal name

R

Raginnis	Ragynys	-Facing the island
Rame		-prob Cornish (meaning unknown)
Ranneys		-Washing rocks (probably from 'ran' dialect for 'run', sea running over them)
Readymoney		-probably personal name or (possibly) 'stone ford'; same name is in Polridmouth
Redannack, Redannick	Redenek	-Fern-brake
Redruth	Rys-drudh	-possibly 'Red ford'
Reen(s)	Run	-Hillsides
Rescorla	Rys-korlann	-Ford of sheepfold
Resparva, Resparveth	Rys-pervedh	-Middle of inner ford
Respryn	Rys-brini	-probably 'crows' ford'
Restronguet	Rys-troen-goes	-Ford on a promontory wood
Resugga	Rys-an-ogo	-Pos. Ford of the cave
Resurrance	Res-Erens	-Ford of Gerens (personal name)
Retallack,Retallick	Rys-Talek	-Ford of Talek (pers. name)
Retire	?Rys-hir	-possibly 'long ford'

Rinsey	Rynnji	-prob. 'House on hillside/promontory'
Rissick	Rys-sygh	-prob. 'Dry ford'
Roche	Tre-garrek	-Rock (French); Cornish = 'Rock Farm'
Roose	Ros	-Heath
Roscarrock	Ros-karrek	-Heath of rock (at Budock Cadoc's heath)
Roscroggan	Ros-krogen	-Heath of limpet shell or of a skull
Roscrowgey	Ros-krowji	-Heath of hovel
Rose	Ros	-Heath or promontary
Rose-an-growse	Ros-an-grows	-Heath of cross
Rosecare	Ros-ker	-Heath of hill-fort
Rosecraddock	Rys-Caradek	-Caradoc's ford; this name is the Ridcaradoch in Geoffrey of Monmouth
Rose-in-vale, valley etc.	Ros-an-avalenn	-Heath of the apple-tree
Roseland	Ros	-Promontory + Eng. 'land'
Rosemellin, Rosemellyn	Ros-melin	-Mill heath
-manowas	-mynowes	-Heath of awl (apparently)
Rose-modress	-Modres	-Modred's heath
-vean	-vyghan	-Little heath
-vear	-veur	-Great heath
-wearne	-wern	-Heath of alders or marsh
-win	-wynn	-White heath
-worthy	Rys-Worgi	-Ford + pers. name
Roskear	Ros-ker	-Heath of hillfort
-killy	-kelli	-Heath of grove
-pannel	-banadhel	-Heath of broom
Rowden		-Rough hill (Eng.)
Ruan Lanihorne		-Ruan, saint's name and Lanihorne,' holy place of Ryhorn'
Ruthdower	Rudh-dowr	-Red water
Ruthvose	Rudhfos	-Red dyke

33

Saint Blazey	Lann-dreth	-Cornish names means 'Holy place on beach'
Dennis	Dinas	-The word meaning hill fort was mis-identified as the saint
Erney		-Actually St Terney
Ingunger	Stumm-gonger	-First part means 'bend'
Ives	Porth Ia	-The saint was called Ia (or Ea): Cornish means 'Cove of Ia'
Levan		-The true name of the saint was Selevan
Sancreed	Sankres	-Name of saint
Savath	Ynys Vargh	-'Island', isolated place belonging to Mark
Saveock	Seviek	-Strawberry patch
Scarrabine	Ros-karrek Byghan	-Little Roscarrock (see Roscarrock)
Sconner	Ros-Konor	-Heath of Conor (personal name)
Scorrier	Skorria	-mining term of obscure origin
Seaton	Seythyn	-Name of river (means 'twisting')
Sennen		-Name of parish saint
Sheviock	Seviek	-Strawberry patch
Sithney		-Name of parish saint
Skewes	Skewys	-Eldertrees
Skewjack	Skewyek	-Place of elder trees
Skillywadden		-Possibly, 'Poor nooks'
Slade		-(Eng.) Shallow valley
Sparnick	Spernek	-Thorn-brake
Sparnon	Spernenn	-Thornbush
Spernen Wyn	Spernenn wynn	-Whitethorn-bush
Splatt		-Eng. dialect 'Plot'
Splattenridden	Splatt-an-reden	-Plot of ferns
Stampas Farm		-from tin-stamps (mining machinery)
Stamps and Jowl Zawn	Saven Stampys-an-jowl	
		-Cleft of the devil's stamps (see above)
Stanbury		-Stone hill-fort (Eng.)
Stenalees	Stenek-lys	-Possibly: Tin-ground of a court
Stencoose	Stumm-koes	-Bend of the wood
Stennack	Stenek	-Tin-ground

Stephengelly	Stumm-an-gelli	-Bend of the grove
Sticker		-probably word meaning 'stile'
Stithians		-Name of parish saint
Streetangarrow	?Stret Garow	-probably 'Rough Street'
Streetanowan	Stret-an-avon	-River street
Street-an-pol	Stret-an-poll	-Street of the pool
Strickstenton	Tre-Gostentyn	-Farm of Constantine

T

Talland	Talan	-possibly from saint's name
Talvan(s)	Tal-vann	-Next to the heights
Tal-y-maen	Tal-an-men	-Next to the stone
Tamsquite	Stumm-koes	-Bend of the wood
Tehidy		-possibly 'House of retreat'
Temple		-from Knights Templar who owned the church
Tideford		-Ford of River Tidy (Tiddy)
Tintagel	Dindajel	-Fort +? personal name
Tolcarne	Tal-karn	-Next to rock-pile
-garrick	-garrek	-Next to the rock
-gus	-goes	-Next to the wood
-pednpenwith	-penn-pennwydh	-Next to the end of Penwith (qv)
-ponds	-pons	-Next to the bridge
Tolskiddy, Tolskithy		-Cor. meaning unknown
Tolvadden, Tolvan	Tal-vann	-Next to the heights
Tor		-(Eng.) 'rocky hill'
Torleven	Tre-leven	-Farm of Levan or Elvan (pers. name)
Torpoint		-(Eng.) 'Tail point'
Towan	Tewynn	-Dune
Towednack		-Name of parish saint
Trago	Tre-Yago	-Farm of Iago
Trannack	Tre-Vranek	-Farm of Branoc

Place names beginning TRE are most often completed with a corrupt form of the name of the settlement's founder. (See BOS). Below are a few with old forms of these personal names:

Treave -	Farm of	Yuf
Trebetherick -	Tre-Bedhrek	Petroc
Trefingey -		Brenci
Tregaddick -dock -		Cadoc
Tregadjack -	Tre-Gasek	Cadoc or Caradoc
Tregassick -	Tre-Gasek	Cadoc

Tregellest -		Celest
Tregenna -		Ceneu
Tregonning -		Conan
Trehaverne -		Gafran
Treisaac -		Isaac
Trelew -		Lew
Treloweth -		Leuueth
Tremellick -		Maeiloc
Tremodrett -	*Tre-Modres*	Modred
Trenithen -		Neithen
Trennick -		Uuethenoc, Guethenoc
Treringey -		Brenci
Tresaddern -		Sadorn
Treseder -		Seder
Tresillian -		Sulien
Tresulgan -		Sulcan
Trethevey, Trethevy, Trethewey -		Dewi
Trethowell -		Dywel
Trevail -		Mael
Trevannion -		Ennion
Trevarthen, -ian -		Arthien
Trevaskis -		Maelscuet
Trevassack -		Madoc
Trevecca -		Becca
Trevedras -	*Tre-Modres*	Modred
Treverbin -		Erbin
Treverbyn -		Erbin
Trevilley -		Beli
Trevillick -		Maelloc
Trevithick -		Budoc
Trevollard -		Maelvargh or Aelward
Trevorrick -		Uuoroc or Moroc
Trewarthenick -		Uuethenoc, Guethenoc
Treweatha -		Uuethen
Trewinnick -		Uuinoc Gwynoc
Trewirgie -		Uuithci, Gwlihgy
Trewithen -		Uuethen, Vueithen
Trewollack -		Uualoc
Treworgans -		Uuorcant, Gorgant
Treworgey -		Uuorcli Gorgy
Treworrick -		Uuoroc
Treath (Helford)	*Treth*	-Passage (ferry)
Trebarvah, Trebarvath	*Tre-bervedh*	-Inner farm
-beigh	*Tre'n byghan*	-Little farm or farm of man
		called An Byghan (Little)
-biffen	*-byghan*	-same as above
-bowland	*-bowlann*	-Farm of cow-pen

36

-bray, brea	-bre	-Farm on hill
-came	-karn	-Farm by rock-pile
-darrup		-probably farm by oaks
-dinnick	Tre-dhinek	-usually probably 'Fortified farm' (at Newlyn East, 'Farm in ferns')
-downs		-probably (Eng.) 'at the down'
-drea	-dre	-'Homefarm'
-drizzick	-dreysek	-Brambly farm
Treen	Tre-dhin	-Farm at fort
Treforda		-probably (Eng.) 'at the ford'
-ffry	Tre-fri	-probably: Farm on a promontory
-gairewoon	-ger-woen	-Farm by the hill-fort on the downs
-gantle	Arghantell	-Silver stream
-garden	-gerdhin	-Farm by mountain ashes (or + personal name)
-garland	-gorlann	-Farm by sheepfold
-garrick	-garrek	-Farm by rock (at St Cleer: Cadoc's Farm)
-garthen	-gerdhin	-see Tregarden
-gear	-ger	-Farm by hill-fort
-gerthen	-gerdhin	-see Tregarden
-gew	-gew	-Farm by enclosed field
-goose	-goes	-Farm by wood
-goss	-gors	-Farm by marsh
Treheath		-(Eng.) 'At the heath'
Trehill		-(Eng.) 'At the hill'
Treheer	Tre-hir	-Long farm
-lanvean	-lann-vyghan	-Farm by the little holy place (or bank)
-lay	-legh	-Farm of the flat stone
-loan	-lowen	-Happy farm, or of someone called Lowen
-lowarren	-lowarn	-poss.Fox farm, or else Farm + pers name
-loarth	-lowarth	-probably Farm of the garden
Tre-loyhan	-leghyon	-?Farm of flat stones
-main, mayne	-meyn	-Farm of stones
Trembath	Tre'n badh/Tre'n bagh	
		-Farm of the boar or of the nook
-bleath	-bleydh	-Farm of the wolf
-braze	-bras	-Farm of man called An Bras (Big)
-broath	-brogh	-Farm of the badger

Tremeer	Tre-veur	-Great farm
-menheere	-men-hir	-Longstone farm
-methick	-an-medhyk	-Farm of the doctor
Trenance	Tre-nans	-Valley farm
-nant	-nans	-Valley farm
-ncrom	'n-kromm	-Farm of the curved hill
-nean	'n-eyn	-Farm of the lambs (or pers. name)
-near, -neere	'n-yer	-Farm of the hens (or pers. name)
-neglos	'n-eglos	-Farm of the church
-newth	-nowydh	-New farm
-ngove, -ngrove	'n-gov	-Farm of the smith (or pers. name An Gof = Smith)
-nithan	'n-eythin	-Farm of the gorse, probably Farm of Neithan, (pers. name)
-noon	'n-woen	-Farm on the downs
-nouth	-nowydh	-New farm
-nowah, -nower	-nowydh	-New farm
-noweth, -nowth	-nowydh	-New farm
Trentinney -	Tre'n-fentynyow	-of the springs
Trenwheal -	Tre'n-hwel	-of the mine
Trenwith -	Trev-ennwydh	-of the ash-trees
Trequite -	Tre'n-koes	-of the wood
Trereen Dinas -	Tre-dhin Dinas	-Farm of the fort: contains two words meaning 'fort'
Trerice-	Tre-rys	-Farm by the ford
-rose-	-ros	-Farm on the heath
-sawsan, -sawser, -sawson	-sowson	-Farm of the English
-scowe	-skaw	-Farm of the eldertrees
Treslay, Treslea	Ros-legh	-Heath or promontory of flat stone
Tresmarrow	Ros-Margh	-Heath or promontory of Mark
Tresparrett	Ros-pervedh	-Inner heath
Trevarrack	Tre-varghek	-?Knight's farm
-vean	-vyghan	-Small
-vear	-veur	-Great
Treveglos	Trev-eglos	-Churchtown
Treven		-(Eng.) At the fen
Trevenna	Tre-venydh	-Hill farm (at Mawgan) Elsewhere probably personal name
Treviglas	Trev-eglos	-Churchtown
Trevisquite	Trev-is-koes	-Farm below wood
Trevose	-fos	-Farm at dyke
Trew	-dhu	-(in Breage) Black farm

Trewartha	-wartha	-Upperfarm
-wavas	-wavos	-Farm at winter pasture
-wen, -win	-wynn	-White farm
-withen	-wydhenn	-poss. 'Tree farm'
-woof	-wov	-The Farm of the blacksmith
-woon	-woen	-Farm of downs
-zance	-sans	-Holy farm
Trink	Tre-frynk	-Frenchman's farm
Trinnick	Tre-dhinek	-Fortified farm
Trungle	Tre-ven-gleudh	-Farm by quarry
Troon	Tre-woen	-Farm on downs
Truro	Truru	-Early forms (Triweru) cannot be interpreted
Trusell, Trussall	Tre-wystel	-Farm of the hostage (prob. personal name)
Tucoyse	Tu-koes	-Side of the wood
Turnaware	Kores-Turnan	-Weir of Turnan (pers. name)
Tywardreath	Chi-war-dreth	-House on the beach or strand
Tywarnhayle	Chi-war-an-heyl	-House on the estuary

V

Valley Truckle	An Velin droghya	-Tucking mill (wool treatment)
Vean	-Vyghan	-Little (first part of name missing)
Vear	-Veur	-Great (first part of name missing)
Vellangoose	An Velin-goes	-The mill in the wood
Vellanoweth	An Velin-nowydh	-The new mill
Vellyndruchia	An Velin-droghya	-Tuckingmill mill (wool treatment)
Vellynsaundry	An Velin-Saundry	-Saundry's mill
Venn		-(Eng) 'fen' marsh
Venton (Ariance)	Fenten (Arghans)	-Spring (of silver)
Venton Ladock	Fenten Lasek	-Well or spring of St Ladock
Venton Raze	Fenten Ras	-Well or spring?of grace
Venton Veor		-possibly 'great spring', but there may be a personal name attached.
Ventonwyn	Fenten-wynn	-White well or spring
Veryan		-Name of parish saint
Vogue	Fog	-Furnace
Voose	An Fos	-The dyke
Vorrap Zawn	Saven Vorrep	-Cleft at seaside (Eng. order)
Vounder	An Vownder	-Lane or cattletrack

W

Warleggan		-Probably a river name
Water-ma-trout		-probably (Enq) 'Water (Wet) my throat' nickname for difficult field?
Week St Mary		-Village of St. Mary
Wendron		-from Gwendern: name of parish saint
Wheal Alfred	*Hwel Alfred*	-Alfred mine
Wheal Bal	*Hwel-Bal*	-Mine works
Wheal Basset	*Hwel Basset*	-Basset mine (name of mineral Lord)
Wheal Kitty	*Hwel Kitty*	-Kitty's mine
Wheal Rose	*Hwel Ros*	-Mine on heath
Windsor, Winsor		-Usually (Eng) Wind's edge
Witheven		-(Eng.) Withy fen
Withielgoose	*Gwydhyel-goes*	-Part of Withiel parish (after patron saint) in wood
Withnoe		-prob. from personal name Guethenoc
Woon	*An Woen*	-The downs
Woon Gumpus	*An Woen gompes*	-Level downs
Wra	*An Wragh*	-The witch or hag

Y

Yeat (e), Yetta	*Yet*	-Gate (Cornish from Old English);

Z

Zawn a Bal	*Saven-an-bal*	-Cleft of the mine
Buzz and Gen	*Saven Bosankan*	-Bosankan cleft
Reeth	*Rudh*	-Red cleft
South	*Soth*	-South cleft
Varrap	*Vorrep*	-Seaside cleft
Vinoc	*Veynek*	-Stony cleft
Zelah	*Syghla*	-Dry place, or perhaps 'a hall' (Old Eng.)
Zennor		-from St Senor
Zone Point	*Penn Saven*	-Point of the cleft